TO PRO

Through the Eyes of an NFL Mom

Part 2

Donna Blueford Stallworth

authorHOUSE®

AuthorHouse™
1663 Liberty Drive
Bloomington, IN 47403
www.authorhouse.com
Phone: 1-800-839-8640

Published by AuthorHouse 9/21/2012

ISBN: 978-1-4772-0593-8 (sc)
ISBN: 978-1-4772-0601-0 (e)

Library of Congress Control Number: 2012910059

Dedication

 This book is dedicated to the memory of my cousin Bobby Cornell Forbes.

Bobby was like my Lil brother/son. He meant so much to me. Bobby knew how important education was. After all, he was a graduate of Clemson University. You could see how important it was by his dedication to helping his sons with their homework. You saw it when he was encouraging his nieces, nephews, cousins and friends. Although Bobby loved sports he was always reminding them that school came first and sports second.

Bobby read my first book titled "From Prep to Pro" Through the eyes of an NFL Mom, and he was looking forward to reading my second and third books.

He always said to me that the books were great and that I was doing a great job getting that information out there to parents and students because it was much needed. He was proud of me. He was always encouraging me and asking me if I worked on my books today?

We were always talking about football in our conversations on a regular bases. I will miss hearing his voice on the other end of the phone. I will never forget that special hug he gave me the night before he passed away. He will be missed by us all.

We all Love you dearly Bobby. R.I.P.

To my grand children: Ke'shaun, Kiana, Nadyca, Larnyz, Londyn and Devaughn whom I love very much. You are all my blessings from God. I am very proud of all of you and all that you've accomplished. You all have done well in school. Continue to stay focused on school and always do the best you can in all that you do. Keep your hearts and minds focused on college, getting a good education and earning a degree.

Ke'shaun, you are the oldest grand child and you are headed to college. You have made some tremendous accomplishments and have done very well. I am very proud of you. Stay focused with your school work. I know you love sports and have done a great job in every sport you've taken on. It's very important to earn that degree so that you will have something to fall back on. If you keep God in your heart and on your mind everything else will fall into place.

Make sure you read the books. You will learn some things.

I love you all dearly. Be Blessed!

This book is also dedicated to Parents, guardians, students, athletes, coaches, and anyone with an interest in leading our young adults, encouraging them, and motivating them to further the achievement of their life goals..

A Letter From Donna's Children

It is a great feeling being children of a very strong, prayerful and powerful woman like our Mother.

"TO PRO" will serve as a guide for athletes who are trying to further their careers and make it to the next level. I urge all of you who are serious about your future to immerse yourselves in reading this book. This book will help you with your journey to pro....

Even if you are in the entertainment business, there is a lot of information in this book regarding finances and different things  you might encounter when you get to that level. If you are a parent or anyone desiring information about agents, the draft, finances, etc, or someone finishing college, you can also benefit from this book. There is a lot of great information in it. This book can be a great asset to colleges, camps, libraries, organizations, foundations, etc. Whether these things apply to you or not, it's still a great book to read.

I wish to congratulate you Mom. You are the GREATEST for keeping your heart and mind on the futures of others. This will no doubt be a great guide to follow for many years to come!

Your son,
Larry Jr.

Mommy, what a wonderful accomplishment to have written your 1st and now 2nd and 3rd books. It has been your goal and dream for years. Just like your books are teaching tools, you always taught us to go with our dreams and visions. You went with your dreams and visions. You never let anything or anyone get in your way. You have always been a very loving and supporting Mother, who educated and loved her children. As an adult I can still say "God has truly blessed me when he gave me to you.

Your Loving daughter
Jamara

We are proud of our Mother for sharing some of her very special parenting skills by way of this book. Our Mother has always told us that she was going to write books after she retired. No surprise to us at all; she continues writing her second and now third books. As with her other books, this book shows our Mother's love, passion, and most of all her ambition to help others make good decisions about their future. This book is not only for young athletes. It contains a lot of great information. I urge you to to pick up copies of this book for college students, libraries, camps etc. Thanks Mom for not only trying to be a Mom and an encourager to others but for encouraging me, loving me and always being supportive of me.

Your 2nd son
Donte' #19 NFL WR

Although the book was not published when I was entering college, all of the information from the book was already known by my Mother, so her knowledge was a great help to me, knowing what to look for and what to expect once I graduated from college and many more topics. You just have to buy the book to see. This book has a "Gold Mine" of information for all parents, college students, and athletes, or anyone who wish to get more information regarding the draft, agents, finances, etc. Now that I have finished college, I am planning my next journey. I have gained a lot of knowledge from this book, so I urge you to pick up a copy or copies of the book. Thanks Mom for all the knowledge and encouragement you've always given me and for all the love you've always shown me.

Your son
Je'von (J.J)

Mother, we congratulate you and we love you very much. We wish you luck in the future with the many more books we are sure you will write.

With love,
Your children

Acknowledgements

I first give all the glory, all the honor and all the praise to God for the gifts and talents that he's given me. I know that if it had not been for the Lord, I would not have written this book. Thank you Lord for Blessing me.

To my children Larry Jr., Jamara, Donte' and JJ, for your encouragement, love and support. Anything I needed help with you were there to help me. My children know the love and passion I have to write books and that this is just the beginning of many more books to come.

To my cousin Bobby Forbes for always encouraging me to write my books and always asking me if I worked on my book today. I wish you were here to see the completion of the books.

To Rhonda Knight, you have been an encourager and an inspiration to me. Thank you for the suggestions you gave me, for everything you did to help me re-write these books, the prayers you prayed for me and the love and support you gave me. I learned a lot from you about the business as an author and a business woman.

Felicia Young, I want to thank you for all the prayers you prayed for me, and the suggestions and ideas you gave me. You've been an inspiration to me. You showed me a lot of things that you've done with your own business as an author that has helped me with my book and business and I thank you for that. You were patient with me and said for me to call you anytime, which I did. I've really enjoyed hanging out with you.

Nina Archie for researching different things for me and being supportive to me and encouraging me. I really appreciated that Nina.

Deanna Moore thank you for the encouragement, motivation and homework assignments you gave me to help me with my 'Prep to Pro speaking engagements. Thank you for all the support you showed me and everything you've shared with me to become a successful business woman. Most importantly, thank you for inviting me on tour and helping me to get started on my journey. Being on tour with your I Think I Can Foundation has given me a lot of exposure which I don't think I would have gotten if it wasn't for the invitation. So I really thank you for that.

Dr. Sirretta Williams you have encouraged me, motivated me and inspired me to do more in the business world. I've learned a lot from you. I really appreciate you taking time out of your busy schedule to talk to me and explain things to me. I see a lot of the work that you've done on your own and I've watched you work day in and day out and still stay on schedule to do more. I just want to say thank you for encouraging me.

To my new quiet friends, Sheryl Howard and Lisa Randolph. Although you two ladies didn't talk much during our events, once we all got together we all had a good time and enjoyed each others' company. You both have a lot of good information to share, so don't be shy. I really appreciate your kind words of encouragement and your friendships. I look forward to hanging out with you ladies again soon.

Christine Lee, thank you so much for always encouraging me and motivating me. I really want to thank you for believing in me and doing everything you can to tell others about my book and for really being excited for me and always checking on me to see how I'm doing. I want to thank you for promoting me and marketing me.

To Mr. L. Martin and the Asante Award Committee for believing in me and recognizing that the information in my book was deserving of my receiving an Asante award. Receiving that award encouraged me to re-write the book, put more information in it, which allowed me to turn the previous one book into two books.

To Bea Bailey for all the help and information you so kindly and willingly gave me as you too are an author and motivational speaker.. I appreciate you because you don't mind if I ask you the same question more than once. You will answer just like it was my first time asking. You have been very patient and kind explaining things to me and giving me good advice.

Jeffrey Wilson, thank you for believing in me, inspiring me, and supporting me. For going out of your way to tell others about my book and encouraging them to buy it and read it. I also want to thank you for believing in making Prep to Pro come to light and becoming successful.

I want to thank my neighbor Peggy for helping me with the last minute problems I had with my computer programs. I couldn't have completed my books without your help. You and Kurt have always been very supportive to me and I thank you and appreciate you.

To all my family members and friends for all the love you all continuously give me and the support you all always show me in whatever I do. You are all always there to encourage me and to lend a helping hand if I need it. Thank you all so much.

To my church family for your prayers and encouragement, my Pastor Dr. Ephriam Williams for all of your words of wisdom, your teachings through the word of God, and your prayers.

To all of you I say "Thank you".

Acknowledgements to Authorhouse

I really would like to thank the teams that I worked closely with at Authorhouse to make this book into what it is today.

Tim Murphy was the representative I spoke with when I first called Authorhouse to inquire about their services. He was so patient and answered all of my many questions. He took time to explained the process and the steps I would take to get the book published. *Faith Allen* was my check-in coordinator. She was patient, kind and a hard worker. We worked diligently together.

J.R. Turner was my Design consultant and he was very patient and kind. He didn't rush me with anything. He explained things to me before we proceeded to the next step. He made sure that we both understood each other before we moved onto the next step. I thought it was great when he congratulated me on the completion of the book.

Teri Watkins was also with the design team. She too was very helpful and she made sure that I had the right forms and explained them carefully to me.

Greg O' Connor was the marketing consultant and he gave me great tips about marketing.

Adalee Cooney for your committment to helping me by working closely with me and for your suggestions. Thank you for your patience and your kindness.

Last but not least I'd like to thank the book consultants for helping with the completion of my book. So again to you all I say "Thank you".

Hearing the words "Congratulations" confirmed to me that I had once again made another great accomplishment in my life. God gets the glory for it all!

Foreword

 Congrats, you are reading "To Pro" that means you are well on your way to doing what is necessary to secure your future. This book is amazing; it is well thought out and well designed. Each chapter is specifically formatted to give you guidelines in a strategic way that will propel you forward and give you an added advantage over others who do not have the wonderful nuggets for success captured here.

The Author offers insight into what to do from the very beginning and lays out for you what is needed step by step. She has thoughtfully considered every obstacle that could or will present itself. With her knowledge and expertise, you are in excellent hands that guide you along your path to success. Pay attention to everything this book has to say, it is not just a theory of what "could" work rather a structured format of what has worked in the past to develop well-rounded players on the field and off.

In the future, look for more of Donna Blueford Stallworth's books, no matter what the subject matter is, you will be moved, educated, inspired and impressed with the contents and gifted ability that this soon to be world renowned Author has within her.

Lastly, as I was reading this book, I saw visions of just how far this book "To Pro" would go and how effective it would be, uplifting and inspiring youths and parents alike.

Evangelist Rhonda Knight,
International Author and Motivational Speaker

The book was a huge help to my husband David and I. We have been blessed with 2 sons that were drafted into the NFL in the 2011 draft. When they were being recruited both in the same year for college we had no idea what to expect and had to learn as we went. It was a blessing to able to use your book as a guide through the NFL draft process. It helped us to interview the many agents that sought after our sons by giving a detailed list of questions to ask and specific warning signs to look for. One of our sons read the book and said he benefitted from it greatly. Although we were completing the college phase of their careers when the book was published I would encourage any parent that has a child who is serious about sports to use the book as a manual to guide them through the process that will hopefully take he/she as far as they want to go.

Thank You,
La Genia Carter

Sons: David Carter Arizona Cardinals
Chris Carter Pittsburgh Steelers

Reading the book truly helped prepare my family and I for the life that we where about to be entering into. With my brother and I both making the transition from college to the NFL at the same time, things got crazy, emotional, and moved extremely fast, but fortunately this book served as a handbook to help slow things down and make sense of it all.

It's a quick read and has great application pages. I recommend that whoever is going through this process or intending on it, definetly read this book.

Chris Carter
OLB Pittsburg Steelers

This is a must read book, especially if you want to be an athlete or pursue your dreams. Donna has allowed her experiences in being a woman of God to become, a fantastic mother, because she loved and nurtured her children into great successes and through this book showed how ambitious she really is.

This book will help you to have faith in your dream and to pursue it by having an education and a Plan B. She never gave up, it should tell moms and dads to search out your children gifts and talents and start seeking God about His plans for them and begin to dream. Everything she said in this great book is true. It pretty much tells how God equipped us to be where we are today. Thanks Donna. Great Job in sharing! It is very helpful. God Bless you on your journey or the dream that God gave to you.

Ms. Felicia Young, The mother of Vincent
Young, Jr. #10 QB NFL

As parents, one of the things we want for our children are lives better than ours. We know that our children's gifts are of God and that it is our obligation to see that these gifts are fully developed. With this in mind, all of the choice/decisions made regarding "the next step" are throughly scrutinized, prayed upon, over pondered, and second guessed.

This book has provided an impetus for students, athletes and their parents transitioning to their next level. Questions are being answered and guidelines are suggested which can be individualized to one's situation.

This information serves as a reference, "GPS" or a blueprint of sorts in preparation for and while experiencing the actual transition from the beginning to the rank of professional. The sequences discussed in the book have not waivered, therefore, having this resource can be likened to having a friend hold your hand and walk with you through life altering processes. It gives you enough insight to know when red flags should go up and when/what things happen next.

After reading the books, not only were we able to assist our son in the collegiate decisions but we were also empowered enough to assist him as he began his career in the NFL.

Cudos, Donna for arming us with the pertinent information to achieve success.

Barry & Orphelia M. Shaw
Parents of Jarrod Shaw Cleveland Browns

It's a great book!!! I think students should be required to read & study this book. It's very imformative and the imformation is clear! If I would have read this book prior to going to high school, I know for a fact it would have had a major impact on how I selected the school to attend, as well as what I should have been looking for in a good college or university.

More importantly, it would have helped my parents, who knew nothing about the NCAA!!

Thanks,
Mike Mckenzie
Retired New Orleans Saints Cornerback

You Can Make a Difference.
Donate. Volunteer. Be a Sponsor.
Teaching, Reaching and Educating Youth 4 Life

My Thoughts as the Author

As I write this book "TO PRO" Through the Eyes of an NFL Mom, I again put on my "MOM HAT" as though I were speaking to my own children. My concern for you as you become successful grows stronger. Our children are STILL our children but by the time they reach the "PRO LEVEL" they should be on their own. They are ADULTS. They want to make their own decisions. Some of them don't want any one giving them advice because they know it all.

My first question is do you have a degree? If not do you plan on finishing school so that you CAN earn your degree within the next couple of years? How many of you have promised your parents that you'd return to college to get your degree if they agreed to let you leave school early to play professional sports, become an entertainer, or to just take a break from college and you have not kept your commitment to them? Shame on you if you're that person. I know someone like that. You still have time to go back to school and get your degree.

As you read this book, you will find a lot of information about finances. Whether you are an professional athlete or an entertainer, some of you are about to make more money than you've ever seen. Are you really ready to handle having all that money?

At this stage of the game I would hope that you are independent, and at the same time, responsible, yet not too GROWN to LISTEN and LEARN. We can never be too BIG or too OLD to learn something. I always say you learn something new everyday. Will you be able to make wise decisions with your money? Will you have control over your money or will your money control you? Will you make money or will your money make you? If God was in your life before you started making a lot of money, Will you keep God in your life once you start making a lot of money or become "rich and famous" or will you not need him anymore? This book will provide you with some financial information.

As you read this book you will also notice that I am also providing you with information regarding agents, finances, how to prepare for the draft, things you might encounter once you get to the pro level, etc. If you pay attention to what I've written in this book, you and your family will have less to worry about. I want you to be successful. I want to see you prosper. That's what inspired me to write the book "TO PRO" Through the Eyes of an NFL Mom.

CONTENTS

Introduction

To Pro

THROUGH THE EYES OF AN NFL MOM

This book titled "TO PRO" is actually part two of the "From Prep" book. Hopefully if you are reading "TO PRO" you've already read my "FROM PREP" book. If you haven't then I would highly recommend that you go pick up a copy for yourself or for someone you know, who might need encouragement or even guidance when it comes to preparing to go college. I also try to help parents understand how important it is to get involved more with their children and encourage their children to get a higher education.

This "TO PRO" book takes the young adult to a higher level which is the PRO level mainly pertaining to sports but at the same time giving great financial advice regardless of whether you're an athlete or not. This book also comes with a journal.

Keep in mind that you don't have to be a professional ATHLETE to be a "PRO." You could be a good financial advisor, a doctor, a lawyer or an entertainer and be called a "PRO" because you've made it to the professional level.

Part 1:
TO PRO

Chapter 1

Your Formula for Success

A PLAN AND A GOAL

Whatever you do in life, you must have a PLAN and a GOAL. Write it down. You're never too young or too old to do this. It's important that you know where you see yourself heading.

Do you have a plan A and a plan B for your life? If you are pursuing a professional sport do you have a plan B in case you don't make it in that particular sport? Will you have something to fall back on if plan A does not work or is short lived?

TAKE A MOMENT TO WRITE DOWN YOUR GOALS AND YOUR PLANS FOR YOUR LIFE FOR THE NEXT 5 TO 10 YEARS.

MY PLANS FOR THE NEXT 5 YEARS

MY PLANS FOR THE NEXT 10 YEARS

MY GOALS FOR THE NEXT 5 YEARS

MY GOALS FOR THE NEXT 10 YEARS

WHERE DO YOU SEE YOURSELF IN THE NEXT 5 YEARS?

Chapter 2

Pursuing a Career in Professional Sports

Listed below are a few reminders when pursuing a career in professional sports

- Signing a professional contract will normally terminate an athlete's eligibility for a scholarship in any sport.

- If you agree formally or in writing with an agent to represent you or market your athletic ability in a sport you become ineligible in that sport.

After my son completed his Junior year, he decided that he wanted to enter the draft. I kept telling him that I would prefer that he stay in school and finish his senior year and get his degree, but I could clearly see that in his own little heart he had his mind made up. So he filled out the necessary paperwork to leave school, and sent the NFL the required paperwork making him eligible to enter the draft. By this time I was putting pressure on him thick to stay in school. After returning to campus, while cleaning out his locker he had a change of heart to stay in school and start his senior year before the January deadline. He wanted to get reinstated back into school and he needed to get an approval from the NCAA.

Since the NCAA refused to restore his eligibility and the NFL had given him an approval to enter the draft, he decided not to file an appeal.

We could've written a letter of appeal but we had no idea of how long it would have taken before we heard anything back from them. We also didn't know if the NCAA would deny him again or if he would have gotten suspended from playing a few games so my son and I had a long talk. I let him make the final decision. He decided to enter the NFL draft. He didn't want to wait a long period of time for them to make a decision and school had already started. Rather than have him miss days from school and who knows how many games he'd be suspended from, I agreed with him and supported his decisions. I still wanted my son to go back to school at some point to finish his classes so that he could receive his diploma.

Not all professional sports have the same rules regarding entering a professional sport. Check with your college or institute regarding the NCAA rules for leaving school early.

HERE'S AN EXAMPLE:

In the sport of basketball you may enter a professional league's draft without jeopardizing your eligibility in that sport, as long as you didn't get drafted. You must also within 30 days declare in writing to your college/institution's director of athletics of your intention to resume playing basketball at the college level.

Keep in mind that if you've violated any NCAA rules, enter the draft and get DRAFTED, don't be surprised if some sort of action is taken once you get to the professional level and get on the roster . A few examples might be a fine or suspension of a few games. Make sure that you know what the NCAA rules are pertaining a particular sport before you decide to enter any draft and if there will be consequences afterward.

Chapter 3

Professional Sports

If you are interested in playing Professional Sports, and you'd like to contact an organization, a league, an association or just need more information regarding a particular Professional Sport, (Men and Women Sports) the directory below should get you to the right organization.

I know a lot of people who play professional sports and I also know a lot of athletes who are interested in playing sports at the professional level, so I decided to included information regarding different professional sports organizations in case someone who is reading this book is interested in contacting one of them.

ON THE NEXT PAGE, YOU WILL FIND A DIRECTORY OF PROFESSIONAL SPORTS ORGANIZATIONS
(Use the space to the right to make notes)

BASEBALL

Leagues:

Major League Baseball
Office of the Commissioner
245 Park Avenue, 31St Floor
New York, New York 10167
212/931-7800
www.mlb.com

Minor League Baseball
201 Bayshore Drive S.E.
P.O. Box A
St. Petersburg, Florida 33731
727/822-6937
www.minorleaguebaseball.com

Major League Baseball Players Association
12 East 49 St.
24th Floor
New York, New York 10022
212/826-0808
www.bigleaugers.com

BASKETBALL

Leagues:

National Basketball Association
645 Fifth Avenue
New York, New York 10022
212/826-7000
www.nba.com

Women's National Basketball Association
645 Fifth Avenue
New York, New York 10022

212/826-7000
www.wnba.com

Continental Basketball Association
1412 W. Idaho St., Suite 235
Boise, ID 83702
208/429-0101
www.cbahoopsonline.com

Organizations:

USA Basketball
5465 Mark Dabling Boulevard
Colorado Springs, Colorado 80918-3842
719/590-4800
www.usabasketball.com

Women's Basketball Coaches Association
4646 B Lawrenceville Highway
Lilburn, Georgia 30247
770/279-8027
www.wbca.org

National Basketball Players Association
2 Penn Plaza, Suite 2430
New York, New York 10121
212/655-0880
www.nbpa.com

FOOTBALL
Leagues

Arena Football
Office of the Commissioner
105 Madison Avenue, 9th Floor
New York, NY 10016

212/252-8100
www.arenafootball.com

Canadian Football League
50 Wellington St. E
3rd Floor
Toronto, Ontario, Canada M5E 1C8
416/322-9650
www.cfl.com

National Football League
410 Park Avenue
New York, New York 10022
212/450-2000
www.nfl.com

Players' Associations:

Canadian Football League Players Association
603 Argus Road
Suite 207
Oakville, ON L6J 6G6
905/844-7852
www.cflpa.com

National Football League Players Association
2021 L Street N.W.
Suite 600
Washington D.C. 20036
202/463-2200
www.nflpa.org

GOLF

Ladies Professional Golf Association
100 International Golf Drive
Daytona Beach, Florida 32124-1092

904/274-6200
www.lpga.com

Professional Golfers' Association Tour
112 PGA Tour Boulevard, Sawgrass
Ponte Verdra Beach, Florida 32082
904/285-3700
www.pgatour.com

Professional Golfers' Association of America
100 Avenue of the Champions
P.O. Box 109601
Palm Beach, Florida 33410
561/624-8400
www.pga.com

ICE HOCKEY
Leagues

National Hockey League
1251 Avenue of the Americas
47th Floor
New York, New York 10020-1198
212/789-2000

and

75 International Boulevard, Suite 300
Rexdale, Ontario, Canada M9W 6L9
416/798-0809
www.nhl.com

American Hockey League
One Monarch Place
Springfield, Massachusetts 01144
413/781-2030
www.theahl.com

East Coast Hockey League
103 Main Street, Suite 300
Princeton, NJ 08540
609/452-0770
www.echl.org

Central Hockey League
4909 East McDowell, Suite 104
Phoenix, Arizona 85008
480/949-8600
www.centralhockeyleague.com

United Hockey League
1831 Lake St. Louis Blvd.
Lake St. Louis, Missouri 63367
636/625-6011
www.theuhl.com

National Hockey League Players Association
777 Bay Street, Suite 2400
Toronto, Ontario, Canada M5G 2C8
416/408-4040
www.nhlpa.com

SOCCER

Major League Soccer
110 East 42nd Street
10th Floor
New York, New York 10017
212/450-1200
www.misnet.com

United States Soccer Federation
1801 South Prairie Avenue
Chicago, Illinois 60616
312/808-1300
www.ussoccer.com

Women's United Soccer Association
6205 Peachtree Dunwoody Road
15th Floor
Atlanta, Georgia 30328
www.wusa.com

SOFTBALL

National Pro Fastpitch
90 Madison St., Suite 200
Denver, Colorado 80203
303/316-7800
www.profastpitch.com

TENNIS

Association of Tennis Professional
201 ATP Tour Boulevard
Ponte Vedra Beach, Florida 32082
904/285-8000
www.atptennis.com

International Tennis Federation
Bank Lane
Roehampton
London
SW15 5XZ
United Kingdom
+44 (0)20 8878 6464
www.itftennis.com

U.S. Professional Tennis Association
USAPT World Headquarters
3535 Briarpark Drive, Suite One
Houston, Tx 77042

713/978-7782
www.uspta.org

U.S. Tennis Association
70 West Red Oak Lane
White Plains, New York 10604
914/696-7000
www.usta.com

WTA Tour
One Progress Plaza
Suite 1500
St. Petersburg, Fl 33701
727/895-5000
www.wtatour.com

TRACK AND FIELD

USA Track and Field
One RCA Dome
Suite 140
Indianapolis, Indiana 46225
317/261-0500
www.usatf.org

NCAA
National Collegiate Athletic Association
P.O. Box 6222
Indianapolis, Indiana 46206-6222
317/917-6222
www.ncaa.org

CONTACTS

CONTACTS

Chapter 4

Off the Field

GET ORGANIZED

The first thing you'll need to do to give yourself the best chance at success at the pro level is have your off field professional life organized. This starts with having a good team to support you, your "off field team." That off field team will start with your agent.

AGENTS IN THE NFL

An agent in the NFL is someone who markets your football skills to the NFL teams or professional teams. They are certified as NFLPA contract advisors. Each agent who is certified will be listed in a book that you can obtain from the NFLPA. This information is also available online. A good agent is honest and knows how to negotiate in good faith, understands what their job is and will represent you well. A good agent will listen to you.

REMEMBER, you hire them; they don't hire you. They work for you. You don't work for them. Normally, agents charge 3% for their services as an agent. Some might charge more. A different amount will be charged for marketing.

Also keep in mind that regardless of the professional sport you are playing, there are some agents who have clients that play different sports. An example would be an agent's clients are professional basketball players and pro football players, or an agent might just represent professional baseball players only, and not represent pro football or pro basketball players at all.

A GOOD AGENT:

- Is honest and will negotiate a contract

- Represents you, knows you, markets you

- Focuses on the present and the future

- Stays in contact with you

- Prepares you for the combine

- Prepares you for the draft with workouts, trainers, nutritionist

- Believes in you

- Makes themselves available to you when you need them, and will come to see you whenever necessary

- Includes your family

INTERVIEW

You interview agents to decide which one you would like to hire to represent you. I SAID INTERVIEW. Don't just sit there like a "bump on a log" and not ask questions. It's an interview. You want to find out all you can about them and how well you think they would represent you. How well do they know how to negotiate a contract in good faith? Always keep a pen and paper handy when interviewing agents so that you can take good notes during the interview and later you can review your notes. If another family member or friend goes with you, then you should both take notes so that you can compare them later.

Once you decide to enter the draft, an agent will either approach you or you can approach them. Usually they will invite you to a meeting at a restaurant, or invite you to their office. If you decide to go to their office and it's in a different state or town, they will usually provide transportation and accommodations for you.

The agent will most likely have a nice presentation for you and your portfolio. This portfolio will include your pictures, stats and a description of the type of player you are, and "will be." The agent may also show you pictures of players they represent. If you go to their office, don't become so impressed with the office that you don't listen to what they are saying to you. Likewise, don't always judge agents by what their office looks like. Keep an open mind, and don't hire the first agent you interview on the spot.

You should visit more than one agent and compare them. This process will help you to decide how well you think an agent will represent you, and how well they would be able to negotiate a contract for you.

Sometimes an agent might work alone and will refer you to someone else to serve as your booking and finance agent. Other agents have ONE-STOP SHOPPING. Be careful about putting ALL OF YOUR EGGS IN ONE BASKET. For example, the agent might be a good choice, but the tax preparer might not be skilled or may not be interested in what is best for you. This can result in financial losses and unexplained charges and transactions. OOPS! So, if you decide to do ONE-STOP SHOPPING, be sure you meet EVERYONE, and find out each staff member's role and responsibilities. This enables you to know exactly who to contact for any information you may need and at any time. REMEMBER: IF YOU DISCOVER THAT SOMEONE IS "MESSING OVER YOUR MONEY" DO NOT LET THEM GET AWAY WITH IT.

Some of the various reputations of agents that you may hear are:

- Better at negotiating rookie contracts than veteran contracts

- Know more general managers, owners and coaches than others

- Has more clients

- They are more popular

- Have football and basketball clients

- Have backgrounds as lawyers but don't necessarily know all about law

- They are more honest than others

QUESTIONS TO ASK AN AGENT

Below you will find questions you might consider asking an agent, or it will give you some ideas of what to ask an agent just in case you are not sure what to say during your interview.

Depending of the sport, some of these questions I've listed may or may not pertain to you. Feel free to choose the ones that do.

- Are you certified?

- How long have you been an agent?

- What is your educational background?

- Did you take the insert players association test? If so what was your score?

- Do you have a law degree? If so what area of law is your specialty.

- Are you married? Do you have any children?

- What athletes do you represent and how long have you represented them?

- Are you still representing them? If not, why?

- Who would you consider to be your top athletes?

- Why are you interested in me?

- What have you done for your clients to advance their careers on and off the field?

- How many staff members do you have?

- Are you a firm, an agency, a partner, or just an employee?

- Do you own your company?

- What services does your company offer or provide?

- Do you have an assistant? What are their names?

- Does your company have a public relations or marketing department? If so what can they offer me?

- What endorsements have you dealt with?

- Do you provide annual statements? If so may I see a sample of one please?

- What percentage do you charge as an agent? Are your fees negotiable?

- How long does the agreement last?

- In what increments do you get paid?

- Do you take a percentage of my signing bonus or my roster bonus if I have one? If so how much, or what percentage will you receive?

- How about endorsements if you were to get some for me, would you receive a percentage of any of that? If so how much or what percentage?

- Where will you send me for workouts? Will I have to pay for the workouts?

- What happens if I don't get drafted, don't make the team, get waived or I get injured?

- What about disability insurance? Would it be necessary to buy it, and exactly how does disability insurance work?

- If I am more likely to be a free agent what can or will you do to help me make a team?

- If I'm not drafted will I pay the same fee as someone who gets drafted?

- Do you have any connections to the other leagues? How much will your fee be if I go that route?

- Does the NFL offer retirement benefits or 401K's?

- Does the NFL contribute any money towards my retirement account? If so how much?

- How many years do I have to play in the league become I become fully vested into my retirement account?

- Is social security taken out of my paychecks?

- Is it necessary to have a foundation? If so could you supply me with information or refer me to someone that could help me get it started please?

- How would you negotiate my contract? Would you be the person negotiating it or would someone else be doing it?

- In your opinion how high is my stock in the draft?

- Is there a tax consultant in your office?

- If I use your agency to do my taxes and I get audited, how much will you back me up and how much will you personally be responsible for if a mistake was found to be on your part?

- Is there an attorney in your office? If so is that part of a package deal you offer to your clients or would I have to pay extra for attorney fees?

- If I got into trouble and needed an attorney would you or someone in your office be able to assist me?

Ok, so there you go. You might have your own questions you may want to ask an agent or you may have additional questions that are important to you. Try to have a set list of questions to ask every agent you interview on separate pages with each agent's name on the top of the page. This makes it easier to compare agents when reviewing your notes. You might even choose to ask the same questions to each one, but there is always going to be one or two different questions for each agent because no two agents are the same.

IT IS VERY IMPORTANT TO ASK OTHERS WHO KNOW THE AGENT ABOUT THEIR REPUTATION.

IF THEY ARE PAST CLIENTS OF AN AGENT FIND OUT THE REASON WHY THE AGENT DOESN'T REPRESENT THEM ANYMORE.

QUESTIONS TO ASK AGENTS AND THEIR ANSWERS

QUESTIONS TO ASK AGENTS AND THEIR ANSWERS

QUESTIONS TO ASK AGENTS AND THEIR ANSWERS

QUESTIONS TO ASK AGENTS AND THEIR ANSWERS

QUESTIONS TO ASK AGENTS AND THEIR ANSWERS

QUESTIONS TO ASK AGENTS AND THEIR ANSWERS

SIGNING AN AGENT

Once you sign with an agent and they negotiate your contract, it's important to note that they will get paid before you do. Hopefully you will get along with your agent and have a good relationship. My advice is to trust your agent, as long as they are trustworthy.

These are some of the qualities I think a GOOD AGENT who is concerned about the well-being of his/her client/athlete has:

- Knows how and will market athlete's football skills to NFL teams or professional teams

- Protects athlete's contractual rights

- Helps athlete earn extra income from endorsements, commercials, etc.

- Allows athlete to concentrate on playing and becomes an advocate for them

- Has knowledge of athlete's strengths and weaknesses

- Knows where the athlete fits in with each team

- Knows the needs of each team

- Converts athlete's skills into financial security

- Will offer financial guidance regarding budgeting, taxes, investments, buying a home, cars, etc.

- Offers educational incentives and will encourage the athlete to return to school

- Will still encourage the athlete to finish school even though the agent can't claim a percentage of the educational payment (if there are fees) as part of their own fees

- Has a good referral source of medical specialists, hospitals, rehab centers, nutritionists and drug and alcohol treatment centers

- Stays updated on players salaries

- Has good rapport with owners, general managers, and coaches

- Will call frequently to check on the well-being of the athlete

- Reviews athlete's needs annually and whenever necessary

- Listens to athlete's concerns

- Feels comfortable talking to athlete and vice versa

- Observant, attends games occasionally

- Requests second medical opinion whenever necessary

- Is Certified

PLANNING FOR A FINANCIAL FUTURE

Whether you are an athlete, a doctor or an entertainer, you MUST learn to manage your money. Making big money does not automatically make YOU a money manager.

The average professional career last just a few years. Will you have anything to show when your career is over? It would be nice if you take a class in money management. After all, it's your money and you are responsible for what happens to it or how you manage it. I'd like for you to do all you can to make your money last and make it work for you. Like we used to say back in the days, "you should always have something to show for all your hard earned work".

You've had to learn how to set goals, make plans for the future, keep a journal, and now I'll attempt to help you manage your money.

It is advisable that you work with a FINANCIAL EXPERT/ ADVISOR. They can help you with investments, annuities, bank accounts, savings accounts, mutual funds etc. They can also assist you in maintaining a PERSONAL BUDGET. They will set up a portfolio for you and explain to you what a portfolio is. If they don't then ask!!!.

FIRST THINGS FIRST

What are your financial needs? Would you respond by saying housing, transportation, clothes, furniture, appliances? Maybe not in that order because some of you would probably have transportation before housing. I probably would too because you can't go looking at houses if you don't have transportation. Did you notice that I didn't list jewelry? That's because we're talking about FINANCIAL NEEDS!!! Not your desires or wants.

If you plan to invest your money make sure your financial advisor explains everything to you. Also make sure that YOU learn about mutual funds, certificates, treasury bills, stocks, bonds and annuities. What they are and how it works. Where to invest and where not to invest. YOU MUST TAKE THE TIME TO LEARN ABOUT THIS.

Make sure that your financial advisor is willing to provide for you full access of your accounts and account records upon your request at anytime and that the advisor is available to you at all times.

Make sure that you fully understand the agreement you make with the advisor and that you understand their financial management and investment stategies.

Make sure that the agreements made between yourself and the advisor is in writing. You might even want to take the agreement to an attorney for review before you sign anything.

Make sure you require the advisor to provide proof of coverage for fidelity insurance or bonding to protect you in case of theft by the advisor.

Make sure your advisor provide you with written reports on your finances on a regular basis.

Important Information to Remember if You are an Athlete:

Signing a professional contract and a signing bonus is a lot of money. Probably more than you've ever had in your life. About 40% of your money will automatically go to pay taxes. Then you have to pay your agent the average 3% fee.

YOUR MONEY

You should learn all you can about anything you do that involves YOUR MONEY. Some players mismanage their money or allow the wrong person to manage it for them. After only playing for a few years their money is gone and so is everybody who wanted handouts. Where are they? They are probably nowhere to be found.

If you make the same mistakes as some athletes and never get an opportunity to play again, you'll spend your time talking about how you "used to be" a great athlete. Then there are others who know that it's time to move on. They didn't make a lot of money, but they do have degrees and can make a living for themselves and their family. Regardless of how much money you may make, you always have to be aware of what is being done with it.

Parents who are working before their child plays pro-sports should also use good judgment, and let it be a family decision between the child and the parents about whether the parents should retire. It's really no one else's business how long, how little, or how much the parent should work. You may often hear people commenting, implying that since the child is making a lot of money the parents don't need to work, or asking the parents how long until they retire. Many people ask such questions out of jealousy and envy and, of course, others are innocently curious.

Always have an extra pair of eyes on YOUR MONEY, including your own eyes. Have someone you can trust to look out for you. It's not always a good idea to hire an agent who does everything for you. It looks good and sounds good, but if you are not paying attention someone could be robbing you and you would never know.

Be careful about totally trusting agents and not confiding in your family, a trusted family member or a friend. Some agents may take advantage of the fact that you are in it alone. So don't stand alone, because you could get "ripped off" if you hire an agent who takes advantage of young men who aren't informed, especially if the agent knows you are a big spender and don't check your balances or keep track of your financial transactions.

NEVER give an agent POWER OF ATTORNEY over all of your finances. If you do that's what they will have, POWER over everything. Be careful about this. If you decide to give an agent power of attorney, be absolutely sure that they are 100% trustworthy.

Do your homework. If you are buying a house, know what your

credit score is ahead of time and get prequalified. Look over all paperwork before signing it. DO NOT, I repeat, DO NOT SIGN ANYTHING IF YOU DON'T FULLY UNDERSTAND IT AND DO NOT SIGN ANYTHING WITHOUT READING THE FINE PRINT. THIS IS VERY IMPORTANT!

REMEMBER...

- Learn as much as you can about:

- Money management

- Contracts

- Agents

- Taxes

- Buying a house/car {interest rates, insurance}

- Flood/earthquake insurance

- Money market/CD's (not music)

WRITE DOWN ALL THE QUESTIONS YOU WOULD LIKE TO ASK AN AGENT AND LEAVE ENOUGH SPACE FOR ANSWERS.

TAKE YOUR TIME AND IF YOU DON'T UNDERSTAND AN

Answer, Ask Again. If You Interview More Than One Agent, Ask Them All The Same Questions, And Then You Can Compare Answers.

Write Their Names At The Top Of The Questionnaire So You Will Know Which Questions Were Asked To Whom.

After You Choose An Agent, Keep The Notes On The Others In Case You Decide To Change Agents. It Is Wise To Keep The Questionnaire Handy To Make Sure The Information Presented During Your Visit Is Still Accurate Once You Sign With Them.

KEEP A JOURNAL

Whether you are talking to your agent, the finance person, or the banker, always write down the questions you want to ask ahead of time. Keep note of the date, the time and the name of the person you spoke with. Don't forget to write down their answers to your questions.

FIRING AN AGENT

If for some reason you don't agree with your agent, or you feel you just need to choose another, you have the right to fire them. This is the procedure in the NFL:

- File paperwork with the NFLPA

- Write a letter to the previous agent. Be courteous, but you don't need to go into lengthy detail. Thank them and let them know you will no longer be in need of their services as of a certain date.

- Make copies of each document for your files.

- You have to wait 5 days after firing your agent before you can hire a new one, so be smart about your timing.

Chapter 5

Contact Information When Preparing for the Draft in Professional Sports

---

In order to have an opportunity to make the roster on a professional sports team, you have to have been drafted, and if not drafted then by signing on as a free agent.

You can determine when or if you'll be drafted by contacting the player personnel scouting services. Your agent will more than likely have this information for you.

Below you will find information regarding draft information for different professional sports.

Football student athletes: contact the NFL'S Undergraduate Advisory Committee for projected ranking in the draft.

Basketball student athletes: contact the NBA for a review of a student athlete's projected draft slot.

The National Hockey League has a central scouting service: They publish a mid-term and final player ranking.

If you don't get drafted there's still a chance to get picked up as a free agent. If you don't get picked up as a free agent you might have to market your skills, try to get invited to try out with a team(club), or get invited to mini camp or training camp to show how good your skills are. You would want to show off your athletic ability in hopes of earning a roster spot on a professional team.

Every year players get drafted into professional sports. It's always been interesting to me to read about the draft requirements for all the different sports since I was always involved in playing so many different sports when I was in high school. I'm going to share some of that information with you.

PROFESSIONAL SPORTS DRAFT INFORMATION

BASEBALL

Major League Baseball (MLB) -- www.mlb.com

The Major League Baseball professional draft is in early June. It consist of a total of 50 rounds in which each team is entitled to make a selection in each of the 50 rounds. Some teams opt not to go that far and cut their draft before their 50th pick.

To be eligible for this draft a player must have to have completed high school, or one year at a two year college, their junior year at a four year college, or their college eligibility. A team has until the beginning of classes to sign a classes to sign a drafted player with college eligibility.

The players that are drafted (and many are college players) don't go straight to their major league teams. Interestingly, it takes time to go from draft day to the major leagues. It sometimes takes years. Even first Rd picks are almost always put into lower ranks and they have to work their way up.

Minor League Baseball -- www.bigleaguers.com

The Minor League Baseball professional draft is the same as the Major League Baseball draft. There is also a professional Rule 5 draft held in December for the players with three or four years of service who are not on a 40 man roster.

BASKETBALL

National Basketball Association (NBA) -- www.nba.com

The National Basketball Association professional draft is held in late June with a total of two rounds. Underclassmen must declare in writing to the NBA to be eligible for the draft. Players living in the United States whose high school class has graduated are eligible for the draft if they renounce their college eligibility by written notice to the NBA at least 45 days before the draft.

National Basketball Development League (NBDL) -- www.nba. com/nbdl

Players eligible for the National Basketball Development League must be 20 years old or older to play in this league.

American Basketball Association (ABA) -- www.abalive.com

The American Basketball Association professional draft consist of six rounds for a first year player draft. There are two rounds of a territorial player draft. There are 12 total rounds, including first year player selections.

Women's National Basketball Association (WNBA) -- www. wnba.com

The Women's National Basketball Association professional draft takes place in May and consist of three rounds. Pre-draft try out camps are a week or two before draft day. Players can participate on other professional teams in the off season.

GOLF

Ladies Professional Golf Association (LPGA) --www.lpga.com

To become eligible for the LPGA, you must contact the LPGA in April or May to request an application. Entries are open to (a) professional golfers who were born female; or (b) amateur golfers who were born female and have a handicap of 3 or less.

Professional Golfer's Association (PGA) --www.pga.com

To become eligible for tournament play, you must:

a) Be in the top 125 from the previous year's money list.

b) Qualifying school: approximately 1,200 players compete.

First and second stage: 72 holes are played to reduce the field to approximately 160 players.

Final stage: 108 holes are played. The top 35 plus ties qualify for the PGA TOUR.

Buy.com Tour

To become eligible for tournament play, you must:

a) Be a winner of tour events in the last or calendar year.

b) Be among the next 70 finishers from the PGA Tour Qualifying Tournament after the top 35 who qualify for the PGA Tour.

c) Be among a minimum of 14 low scorers at open qualifying for each event.

ICE HOCKEY

National Hockey League (NHL) -- www.nhl.com

The National Hockey League professional draft consist of nine rounds in early June. Any amateur who will be 19 years old by September 15 is eligible for that year's draft and any player who will be 18 by September 15 may opt in and be eligible for that year's draft.

Currently any player who elects to opt in losses collegiate eligibility.

If the drafting team offers a contract within one year, the player remains the property of that team for two years. If a drafted player enrolls at a college rather than signing a contract, he remains the property of that team for 180 days after he graduates or leaves school. After age 20, all undrafted amateurs become free agents except Europeans.

Minor Hockey League

Most players in the Minor Hockey League are signed as free agents through recruiting scouts. Some players in the international Hockey League or the American Hockey League may be under the National Hockey League contracts through the "parent club."

SOCCER

National Professional Soccer League (NPSL) -- www.allsports. com/npsl

The National Professional Soccer League draft consist of five rounds each December. Underclassmen must petition the league office in order to be drafted. Any player doing so jeopardizes college eligibility.

Major League Soccer (MLS) --www.mlsnet.com

The Major League Soccer professional draft is conducted in conjunction with a combine sponsored by the MLS and the college all-star game in early February. The draft consist of a six round "Super Draft" including players from project 40 and college seniors. That draft is held in early February in conjunction with MLS spring training.

Women's United Soccer Association (WUSA) --www.wusa.com

There is no professional draft for the Women's United Soccer Association. Each player is assigned by the league.

SOFTBALL

National Pro Fast Pitch (NPF) --www.profastpitch.com

The National Pro Fast League annually drafts the nation's best fast pitched players as well as the top senior collegiate player in the country.

The "elite" draft includes invitees who have completed their collegiate eligibility. The names of the senior collegiate student athletes are nominated by each of the eight team operators.

Women must be 21 years old to compete in the leagues;

The NPF does not sign players to contracts until they have finished their college eligibility.

TENNIS

ATP Tour (Men) -- www.atptennis.com

Players gain acceptance into the main draw of a sanctioned men's professional tennis tournament in the following ways:

a) Direct acceptance based on ATP Tour ranking at the time of entry (accounts for the majority of main-draw players).

b) Wild card (limited number).

c) Qualifying -- All sanctioned tournaments have a qualifying competition, of at least the same draw size as the main draw, before the event. There is one qualifying spot for each eight spots in the main draw.

d) Special exemption.

Sanex WTA Tour (Women) -- www.wtatour.com

To become eligible for membership into the WTA, you must:

a) Have earnings in excess of $35,000 one or more previous years for full membership.

b) Have earnings in excess of $500 in one or more of the previous two years for associate membership.

FOOTBALL DRAFT INFORMATION

The National Footbal League (NFL) -- www.nfl.com.

The National Football League draft consists of seven rounds. The average round has 32 picks, which allows each team approxiamately one pick per round. Some teams have more than one pick in a round, where others may not have any picks in a round. Picks per team vary because draft picks can be traded to other teams, and the NFL can award additional picks to a team if the team losses players designated as restricted free agents.

Underclass players are prohibited from entering the draft until three college football seasons have passed since their high school graduation.

The deadline for underclassmen, sophomores and juniors to declare their eligibility for the NFL draft is in January. Once the players declare for the draft they forego their remaining eligibility to play college football.

The National Football League Europe (NFLE) --www.nfleurope.com

The National Football League Europe professional draft takes place in February each year. The draft consist of 20 plus rounds. Some players may be assigned by NFL clubs while others sign as free agents.

Arena Football League (AFL) -- www.arenafootball.com

All players signed to contracts in the Arena Football League are free agents.

Canadian Football League (CFL) -- www.cfl.ca

The Canadian Football League professional draft is held in late February and consist of six rounds.

Chapter 6

Preparing for the NFL Draft

NFL SCOUTING COMBINES

Every February in Indianapolis, Indiana, at Lucas Oil Stadium, college players perform physical and mental tests in front of National Football League coaches, general managers and scouts. This is by "invitation only," which means the players have to be invited to this combine. It usually lasts one week and is televised. Family members and agents are not allowed inside the stadium. A few of the different skills and tests done at the combine are listed below:

NFL COMBINE TESTS

- Intelligence test (Wonderlic Test)

- Drug test

- 40 yard dash

- Broad jump

- Vertical jump

- Bench Press

- Position- specific drills

- Interviews- by each team

- Physical measurements

- Injury & Physical evaluation

PRO DAYS

There are also combine "PRO DAYS" at each university. Some players might feel more comfortable at their own campuses than at the combine. Prepare yourself for this big important day mentally and physically. Work hard to reach your destiny. Don't eat or drink anything just before your workout that will keep you running to the restroom. Your families are allowed on campus to watch you and support you during your pro day workout. Agents are not allowed to watch. ALL EYES ARE ON YOU so do your best. Get plenty of rest the night before. If you have an agent already, hopefully he has gotten you "hooked up" with an agency that has well-prepared you mentally and physically for the next level in football. It's also a good idea to talk to someone who already been through the preparation process.

Remember that the NFL combine is the FINAL ENTRY on a rookie's football resume.

When my son Donte' had his Pro Day at his college, it was a very exciting day for all of us. I could tell that Donte' was a little nervous but he did a great job not showing it. My oldest son Larry and I tagged along to give him moral support. That day ended up being a great day for him. In the 40 he ran a 4.2 or a 4.19 depending on what your stop watch clocked him at. I will never forget it. After he ran you should have seen all the expressions on people's faces including mine. I was up on the balcony (second floor) so that I could have what I called " a front row seat". A lot of people showed up that day. It was very exciting. I remember calling family members, friends, and co workers to tell them about what I had witnessed.

Pro Day can work different ways for players. It can work for you or it can work against you. It's up to you to make the very best of it. You must continue to disciple yourself and work hard so that you will be well prepared when the opportunity arrives for you on that long waited day. You can't be concerned about anyone but yourself. You have to be prepared. You have to go there with the mental attitude that you are the best player there.

My son JJ didn't get utilized much, playing collegiate football the way he would have liked to, nor was he recognized as a player that scouts would be hunting down. He never even scored a touch down pass in a real game, therefore he didn't really have film to show the scouts and the NFL coaches his true athletic ability. That's when you have to come out strong on pro day. You have to shine. His best bet is to hope that by God's grace and mercy that he gets drafted. You never know exactly how the draft is going to pan out. He ran great routes and caught all the balls that were thrown to him, ran about a 4.5 in the 40 yard dash. The newspaper didn't even mention his name as one of the players that worked out on Pro Day. He ended up with a little hammy injury on Pro Day but he worked through his injury and ended his day strong. I wish him the best of luck.

If he doesn't get drafted or picked up as a free agent, and he's still wanting to play football, he could try out for a team or he could play for the arena football league or one of the other leagues. If all else fails, one thing for sure we know is that he graduated from college and he has his diploma. He has something to fall back on and no one can take that away from him.

YOUR ATHLETIC ABILITY VS YOUR PERSONALITY

Usually, the athletes who have done well, or might be top prospects have to be really careful if they have anything "hidden in their closets". You can be a great athlete and if one incident has occurred; regardless of how insignificant you think it was, it will resurface. Even if you had an injury in high school, you will hear about it. Be prepared because sometimes when you've done something wrong, just when you think you can breathe, or nothing was said about it, BAMM!!!!! There it is. In some cases information was given by a former coach or there's something the media digs up and brings to surface to make a story. These incidences can play a factor in where a player is selected on draft day.

If something does surface you will be asked questions about it. This is the time when the media tries to find out all the negative things about you or a close family member. If you have violated any NCAA rules, or if the media thinks you have, then you can bet your bottom dollar that they will throw as much information as they can out there FOR THE PUBLIC TO SEE AND TO HEAR. Anything they think will draw attention, especially before the draft, will be publicized. Do the best you can to make sure that your personal background information is in good standing. Most of that starts well before you have the chance to go pro, so make good decisions.

Chapter 7

The NFL Draft

The NFL DRAFT is an annual event held in April where 32 NFL teams select new players from the NCAA college system.

Previously it was held in April for only 2 days with rounds 1-2 on Saturday and rounds 3-7 on Sunday. However, beginning in Aprill of 2010 the draft was held for 3 days from April 22 through the 24th. That was the first year the draft was held for three days rather than the previous two days. In 2012 the draft was held from April 26th through April 28th.

- Round 1 was held on Thursday, April 26th

- Rounds 2 and 3 were held on Friday April 27th

- Rounds 4- 7 were held on Saturday April 28th

The 2013 draft will be held the end of April for three days. I don't have any specific dates at this time.

The change in the schedule was made to make the event more accessible to the fans. Draft Day can be a happy or disappointing day, depending on the outcome. Not everyone will be selected for the round they were predicted in, nor will each player be chosen for their preferred spot. An invitation to the draft in New York is not received by all players; only the top prospects will be invited to attend.

AN EXCITING DAY

When my son decided to enter the draft, I decided that I was going to learn as much as I could about everything I thought I was going to be dealing with. He chose an agent who was very informative and whom I felt did a great job preparing him for the combine and the draft. The night before the draft we prayed and we talked about how all of our lives were going to change. We had a lot of support from family, church family, friends and co-workers.

On draft day we were at his apartment with one of the local news stations and someone from ESPN and his agent. It was my birthday so that made it even more special for me. We waited patiently while my son and his teammates played jokes on each other and predicted among each other what teams they were going to. My son and two more of his team mates were drafted in the first round. When he was selected, we cried and hugged each other, and thanked God for his many Blessings.

Immediately following my son's selection we got on a plane to meet with the coaches, owner and GM of the team that drafted him.

We got there in the evening and someone from the team was at the airport to pick us up. We were bombarded by media, news reporters, and fans. We had dinner with the wide receiver's coach, and the next day we had breakfast; followed by a press conference, interviews, introduction to staff and a tour around the facility.. It was a great feeling for both of us. I remember it like it was yesterday. To God be the glory for the things He has already done, is doing now and what He's going to do.

Some will be drafted, some will become free agents, and others will not receive a phone call at all.. If you don't get drafted high, or drafted at all, don't be discouraged. There are many cases of players that have not been drafted and made teams or have been drafted in the later rounds and won Super Bowls. I have witnessed a case where a player was selected late in the draft, but went to camp and did well. He showed up and "showed out" in the pre-season game and eventually got a good contract. Drafted or not, you still have to prove yourself.

SUPPLEMENTAL DRAFT

The NFL supplemental draft has been held since 1977 for players who did not enter the regular draft or missed the filing deadline because of issues which affected their eligibility, such as athletic or disciplinary reasons. The draft is scheduled at some point after the regular draft which is held in the month of April and before the start of the next season. The date varies so please check with your agent or the NFL office.

Only those NFL teams with six wins or less are grouped into the top of the draft, non playoff teams with more than six wins are in the second tier and all 12 playoff teams are in the third tier. Then each team submits to the league a list of players they're interested in and what round in the supplemental draft they would like to draft that player. If a team is the first team in the draft order to bid on a player, they get the right to sign that player. If a team wins the rights to a player, the team must give up a pick in the next year's NFL draft. Whatever round that the team won the supplemental draft player in is the same round that team will lose in their next season's NFL draft pick.

Teams are not required to place a bid in the NFL supplemental draft. If a team does not win the rights to a player, they will not be required to give up a draft pick in the next season's NFL draft.

DISAPPOINTMENTS AFTER THE DRAFT

After the draft is over, some athletes are devastated for various reasons. Some were not picked up as free agents. Some were and are disappointed in that. Some players go to many teams and are not selected or maybe never perform well at all. Disappointment can cause embarrassment because of the former success in college. All kinds of emotions are experienced by these players. However, some athletes refuse to give up and choose to keep hope alive. My advice is if you really feel in your heart that something is for you, continue to pursue it. You will never know how it will turn out if you don't keep trying. YOU MUST ALWAYS PUT IN TIME AND EFFORT.

I believe in my heart there is a TIME, a SEASON and a REASON for everything. It may not be your time or your season. The purpose might be to change your ways, your thinking or your behavior. Maybe God has something He wants you to do or He may be trying to get your attention. We may not always be able to see clearly or understand fully why things happen or why they end up the way they do. In time you WILL understand.

Family members share the frustrations and disappointments. It is very hard for parents to see their child hurting, because his/her dreams were not fulfilled. This is when a family needs to be supportive. Unfortunately, some parents are only thinking about the money, and the athlete is remembering all their hard work and time spent in fulfilling the dream that did not come true. Parents should never consider their child a failure because things didn't work out according to their plans.

NFL PLAYERS CONTRACT

Unfortunately, all of the NFL players' contracts are not guaranteed like NBA and MLB players, probably because they have to sign more players and it would be too expensive. Certain parts of the contracts are guaranteed from year to year. If a long contract is signed, the last two years will probably not be honored. Make sure your agent explains your contract to you in full detail. Read it thoroughly. Ask questions. Study the structure of the contract. Study dollar amounts. Go over it again and again before signing it. If you do not understand it, don't sign it until you do.

Players' salaries are based on the position drafted for. The high first round picks are paid the highest salaries and the lower rounds are paid less. Free agent rookies aren't paid as much as drafted rookies. Before the draft starts only the teams that have the first overall pick can agree to a contract with a draft-eligible player. Make sure you are well-groomed and wearing a nice suit so you will look professional when you meet your new coach, the general manager, and the owner of your team. As I stated earlier, all players are not drafted or picked up as free agents. That's why it is very important to get a degree so that you will have options. In either case, the game doesn't last forever.

Veteran contracts are structured differently than rookie contracts. The SECOND contract a player receives is one of the most important, simply because it's more money. After an athlete has played for a few years and has been re-evaluated they'll have a chance to negotiate a better contract. Unfortunately, this can be the last contract for some players, either due to injury or under performance.

GETTING TO KNOW THE NEW ROOKIE CONTRACT

If a long contract is signed , the last one or two years will probably not be honored. However, in 2011 due to the new rookie wage scale a lot of changes were made, one being that the rookies make less money than they did the previous years before the new plan and the contracts were shorter in duration meaning instead of signing 5 and 6 year deals they signed 4 year deals.

Under the new plan, all first round selections will now sign a four-year contract with an option for the fifth year. Players that are picked within the top ten will be paid the average of the top 10 highest paid players in that position. Picks 11-32 will be paid the average of the 3rd to the 25th highest paid players at their position.

The length of the new Rookie wage scale contract is listed below:

- 1st round pick's contracts will have a 4 years plus an option for the fifth year.

- Picks in all later rounds will have 4 year contracts.

- Undrafted players will have 3 year contracts.

Make sure that you understand what the team option is for the fifth year if it is excercised, because it can be very confusing:

If the team option is excercised, in the fifth year the top 10 picks would receive a salary equal to the average top 10 player salaries at their respective positions. That money would be guaranteed if the option is excercised after the third year of the contract.

If the team option is excercised, in the fifth year, picks 11-32 would receive a salary equal to the average of the Nos. 3-25 salaries at their perspective positions. That money would be guaranteed if the option is excercised after the third year of the contract.

Do You Understand Your Contract?

Are You Happy With It? Are You Ready To Sign It?

Chapter 8

Rookie Year

This can be a very happy and/or stressful year. Many players are happy because they are on a team and they're receiving a paycheck. It can be stressful for a lot of reasons too. Players may have to work harder than they anticipated or maybe they aren't performing as well as they thought they would. There is always room for improvement. As a drafted rookie, ALL EYES ARE ON YOU. Prove yourself worthy of the contract you received. Be the best you can be. Keep a good attitude on and off the field.

If you are a rookie, this first year alone will involve many experiences and you will have issues to address. You will attend a rookie symposium which will be very informative. Make sure you pay attention to everything that is said. You will find out how to handle your money and your business. Invest your money in a retirement account, you are not too young to start. Make sure you get to know the staff members of your club and the director of player personnel and members of the NFLPA which is the National

Football League Players Association. Whatever sport you're in, get to know the different personnel directors of your league.

You will have to pay taxes in every state you play in. Approximately 40% of your salary will go to taxes, and you might consider setting money aside to pay taxes. Every state is different. If you live in California the taxes are higher because you pay state and federal taxes, but there are a few states in which you will not have to pay state taxes. If you live in Florida or Texas you should check to see if you are required to pay a "JOCK TAX", and find out how much it is. If you play a sport other than football, you should check to see if this tax applies to you.

Chapter 9

Rookie Symposium

All drafted rookies in the NFL are invited to an annual mandatory Rookie Symposium. The purpose of the symposium focuses on helping the rookie transition from college to the pros. It's like an orientation program helping rookies adjust to life in the NFL. The NFL Rookie Symposium is for four days. Guest speakers and experts are brought in to discuss various issues and to raise awareness of the temptations that come along with money and fame. You'll wake up one day and suddenly you'll have more money than you've ever had. You'll get a course on how to handle your money.

The players won't be allowed to leave the premises without permission. They cannot have guest or drink alcohol. Cell phones, pagers, do-rags, bandannas and sunglasses will not be permitted during the proceeding. I really like the sound of the rules implemented for the symposium.

Attendance to the annual Rookie Symposium is not only mandatory but fines will be imposed upon anyone invited who does not attend. Being late or missing curfew will also result in a fine.

I'm just going to talk a little bit about a few other leagues that have programs to help educate the Rookies. I really think these programs are much needed and beneficial. There are some young men that don't think it's necessary because they know everything, but I always say it never hurts to listen and you don't know everything. You might think you do but you don't. I also feel that if you listen closely, you might learn something.

The NBA and the MLB/MLBA have similar programs to the NFL Rookie symposium with the same tactics in mind, helping the Rookies adjust to life at the pro level, informing them of what they could expect in their first year.

The NBA's Rookie Transition Program is held for three days consisting of about 50 incoming rookies, but not all of them will make the roster. They talk about on and off the court challenges, drugs, sex, gambling, everything these young men will/could encounter on their way to celebrity status and fame. They also get lectures from former players and many more guest speakers. Keep in mind that these young men range in ages 19 to 22 years old and they are about to come into a lot of money.

The MLB Rookie Career Development Program is held for four days. Each January major league teams send some of their brightest prospects to Washington DC. It's offered to a few of the top prospects from all

33 ball clubs. They speak on handling life away from the baseball field, lessons in company policies, financial planning, community relations and other important topics. They are lectured to and catered to.

When my son attended his Rookie symposium, he felt that it was very informative. I had a lot of questions for him. I wanted to know what was said, what he learned and if he enjoyed being there. He mentioned that there were different speakers who spoke on a lot of different topics like finances, alcohol, drugs, sex, etc. He talked about the skits that were done. He felt it was benefitial. It also gave him an opportunity to meet other players who were drafted.

ROOKIE PREMIERE

The Rookie Premiere is an event put together by the media to get coverage of the new rookies coming into their respective leagues for photo shoots with jerseys that will be put on trading cards. Every year a group of draft picks head to Los Angeles for the Rookie Premiere.

I think every athlete who attends the Rookie Premiere look forward to a day filled with fun and photo shoots.

FINES

There are a lot of different reasons why a player might be fined by their team or the league. It could be as simple as having your socks rolled down or celebrating on the field. You may also be fined for being late for practice, a game, a meeting or not showing up for meetings without approval. Being fined is taking money out of your own pocket. Why would you allow the same people who give you a paycheck to take it away?

If you are fined for an incident that occurred during a game you have the right to appeal. On the other hand, if you just don't want the money and want to throw it away, I am sure there would be a lot of people standing in line to get FREE MONEY. I assume you work to get PAID.

Just imagine you invested the money you were fined over a five or ten year span. How much money do you think you would have invested? Think about the return and the revenue. We're talking about $5,000 or 10,000 invested versus $5,000 or $10,000 going down the drain. That's give-away money. At the end of the year, you might not be able to donate it to your favorite charity, and it will not be a tax write-off for you.

BLING BLING!

For some reason when some guys make a lot of money for the first time they want to spend it on fancy jewelry before they do anything else with it. Everything is "BLING," watches, necklaces, bracelets, rings, you name it. I love jewelry. It looks nice. However, some of these athletes wear so much you have to wear sunglasses to prevent blindness from the flash. Although you may think it's cool, people can be jealous and want what you have worked hard to get. Be careful when wearing these things in public. Even more importantly, learn to SPEND YOUR

MONEY WISELY and BE AWARE of the dangers that can come when you are a visible professional athlete.

GROUPIES

Believe it or not there are male groupies. No one really calls them that, but they are an obvious group of men who hang around pro-athletes. These groupies want to be their pals, buddies or "Homies" so they can get freebies from them. They want to go everywhere they go, and do everything they do. They often want the athletes to spend their money on them; looking for their "Homie" to pay for their meals, their hotel rooms and all kinds of other things. If you are fortunate enough to earn that money, be careful of who hangs around you.

It's different when these guys are your true friends and care about you. They have their OWN MONEY and no ulterior motives. They pay for their meals, hotel rooms and airline tickets. These are the friends that will warn you about others that may not have your best interest at heart. True friends do not take advantage of one another.

Beware! There are some women out there who just want to date you because you are a paid athlete. You have more money now than you have ever seen. I'm sure you know that some women will do whatever they can to trip you up so they can get pregnant. Others just want you to spend your money on them. Looking good on the outside these women trap athletes. Some of them even convince the athletes to autograph their body parts and the men find themselves being charged with rape.

These women are usually beautiful, or at least appear to be. What looks good is not always good for you.

Some of these guys have a different women with them every week. Each one of these women want to be a part of that fame and fortune. They know these guys have fame and fortune and they want it to. They want to be in the spotlight. A lot of them get their wishes because that's how some men make them feel. They might get their airfare paid to visit these guys and to go to games. Can you imagine how these women are feeling? They are feeling like they are on top of the world. That's why when one man or athlete drop this type of women, it's so easy for her to say "next" and move on to the next guy because they know it will probably be another athlete who will treat them the same way if not better.

Keep in mind that these groupies will hunt a man down if they want to be with him. Trust me, they are doing their homework and they're doing their research on you. They know where you hang out and who you hang out with. They know the hotels you stay at before the games. They sit and watch to see what time you leave and what time you come back. They hang out in the lobby. They flirt with you whether you're married, in a relationship or have your lady friend with you. Sometimes these type of women can be very disrespectful with their actions. They are easy to spot. These women also brag about what they do and they are proud of it. It's their profession. With some of these women this is their only job. The sad part is with these type of women, they can't draw unemployment off of these men. They don't get any retirement or medical benefits. Some of these women try to impress these guys and hope they can marry them. While others are just in it for the fun and the upgrades.

MEN: I want you to know that there are a lot of educated classy women out there if you would just look in the right places for them. I know young ladies who make their own money, have their own cars, their own homes and they aren't trying to make a living off men.

For some reason, and I can't figure it out yet, but I've noticed that some men like needy women. Why? Your guess is as good as mine. I'm not just talking about athletes, I'm talking about some men in general. What I've observed over my years of watching and observing men. This is my own opinion.

Some are airline ticket queens. They will visit guys only when the guys pay for their airline tickets, dinners, hotel rooms and gifts. Some don't mind sharing the man at all with other women. Unfortunately, some men are attracted to these types of women. Although I am "old fashion," there are too many diseases to not take care of your body. It can be a matter of life and death. Men, just because you have money, be careful what you buy, and I am not talking about clothes.

For those of you who are living this type of lifestyle, you may not see it now, but keep living and one day you will look at things differently and realize that the previous lifestlyle you were living is not really cool for you anymore.

Women athletes should also be cautious of men who want them for money and status. Men play mind games too. They lead the ladies on, thinking they have found their man, only to find out they are not even the girlfriend.

DON'T GIVE EVERYTHING AWAY OR WHEN YOU REALLY FIND SOMEONE YOU TRULY LIKE OR FALL IN LOVE WITH, YOU MIGHT NOT HAVE ANYTHING GOOD LEFT TO OFFER THEM.

SAVE THE GOOD STUFF FOR THE ONE GOD SENDS TO YOU AND CHOOSE YOUR MATE WISELY. HAVE RESPECT FOR YOURSELVES.

REMEMBER... AN INDIVIDUAL CAN/WILL DO NO MORE TO YOU THAN WHAT YOU ALLOW.

THINGS YOU MIGHT ENCOUNTER

If you have made it to the pros, by now you have probably heard from people you had not seen, spoken to or heard from in years. There will be family members and friends who will be truly happy for you and there will be those that are upset, jealous and envious. Some will try to start arguments and fights with you or a close family member, and others will choose to never speak to you again. They think you owe them something, such as a car, a house, money or whatever.

In my opinion, you should take care of your immediate family first and then do whatever your heart desires for others. People are quick to imply that YOU HAVE CHANGED. In most cases, those individuals should take a few steps back and open their eyes. They will see that they are the ones who have changed, either because they did not get what they wanted from you or because they are wanting something from you and haven't received it yet.

There are people around you that can be happy for you. They haven't changed towards you and they encourage you to do whatever is placed on your heart for them, and they appreciate it. Those same people still come around and don't expect anything from you. However, everyone who shakes your hand and says that they are happy for you isn't.

People may have asked why they should be happy for you when you haven't done anything for them. There are always people who hope that you won't succeed. They use their energy to go online everyday to see if there is anything negative being said about you so that they can have something to talk about. They want something bad to happen so they can say I TOLD YOU SO or that it was too good to be true. Again, energy has been used on negatives rather than positives. It doesn't make me happy to see anyone fail. So don't let negative people discourage you.

AWAY GAMES

When your team travels away from your home stadium, neither you nor your family should expect good seats unless you know someone on the other team that you can buy tickets from or you buy your own tickets. My advice is don't expect to have good seats everywhere you go. Sometimes there may be people you know that always want tickets to games. That's up to you, but don't forget, those tickets come out of your paychecks. Your parents, your wife, if you're married, your children and your siblings might come first. All of this is really up to you as long as you know you are the one paying for the tickets.

Beware that some people, family or otherwise, might always want tickets but aren't appreciative because they feel that you owe them a tickets. The best thing to do is set rules right from the beginning, and then there won't be as many issues because everyone will know where they stand. Again, it's up to you. You can't please everyone. So don't try.

THE MEDIA

The media can either build you up or tear you down. Don't believe everything you hear or read because the media doesn't always FULLY investigate a story before they print it. Not all people in the media respect your boundaries. Beware of these individuals, because they are quick to print false statements or "create" a story that is untrue. I have even experienced instances where reporters will tell you to give them an interview or else they will make their own story.

Sometimes media will "jump the gun" and write an article before they find out the facts. They simply record "hearsay" and add their "two cents" to juice it up. These reporters are trying to fabricate a story to make headlines and make money. Occasionally you will find reporters and writers that will be honest. They really care about the truth and will write a good article in your defense. Sometimes the reporter will even let you read a copy before it is printed to verify accuracy. Those are the ones you appreciate. The others will always write negative stories because they are negative people and will write anything to make money, even if it's not true. As a professional you have to learn to not let those things bother you.

Some players want to capture all the media attention, and others always seem to draw media attention, whether they try or not. That's cool if that's what they like. Let them do that. Sometimes it's funny. Laughter is good for all of us. In today's society, HIGH PROFILE ATHLETES seem to be the targets of interest. It is as though a certain group of athletes is being targeted more than others. It's important to be mindful that if you are an athlete of high interest, everything you say or do will be under a media microscope. Things will be said about you constantly. The media will look to make news out of anything involving you. This is especially true in your hometown, state of residence and the city and state where you play. If one incident occurs with you, a great deal is made of it. If the media's questions are not answered, they may make their own assumptions. Some of the information may be inaccurate, and although the media knows it, they won't always care. HIGH PROFILE stories sell.

This is not always the rule when it comes to the media. Don't let a few bad apples ruin the whole bunch. I know from experience there are fair reporters looking to do an honest job. Those are the media people you can trust to do the right thing because they are trying to report the truth.

FANS

When you play sports, the fans are the one who buy the tickets and the merchandise. Fans want to enjoy the sport and they want their team to win. It is important for all athletes to respect the people that support the game. Athletes have the opportunity to be part of people's lives and share in memories that will last a lifetime. I always tell my kids not to forget the little ones. When you sign autographs don't just get the ones you can easily reach. Take extra care to pay attention to the young fans. Be respectful and appreciative of that special opportunity and the people that you share it with.

Fans can also be mean and cruel. They will sometimes call you names or say mean things about you or even talk trash about you and they not really know what they are talking about, nor are their stories accurate. They just talk to be heard. Sometimes it starts a chain reaction.

With the new technology of face book and twitter, fans will use them to their advantage to talk trash about you. I'm not saying that all fans do this. Some fans really are true fans and will use facebook and twitter to say things about you that are a little more kinder or to encourage you.

My advise to you is to ignore all negative talk. Don't respond to negativity. Don't even waste your energy level thinking about it. It can be difficult at times but try to stay focused on prosperity and success.

Sometimes athletes will use that same negative talk to hype themselves up. They won't let it distract them. If you get distracted easily by negativity then stay around positive people and think positive thoughts. If the fans say you can't make it, just know that you can. If the fans say you won't succeed just know that you will. Don't let them get to you. If necessary, don't read negative articles. Don't keep reading facebook or twitter if it upsets you. Let everyone know that you're doing your best to stay positive. Shut down all negative talk.

Chapter 10

Decisions

THE OFFSEASON

Most players welcome the off season so they can take a break, go on vacation, return home to another state, or just go home and relax with their families. Celebrating, winding down and sleeping in makes the offseason a special time. However, some players might use this time to have too much "fun". Remember your behavior during off season will also be scrutinized by the media. It's not always where you go but what you do when you get there. Just because it's off season doesn't mean you "party hardy" until the last day. When the new season begins, you need to be in shape mentally and physically and that happens in your offseason preparation. Again, there's nothing wrong with having a good time, just be prepared and in good shape for camp. Give yourself time to adjust to working hours at least a week before you head back to work, especially if you have trouble getting up in the morning.

DRUGS AND ALCOHOL

There are many restrictions and consequences concerning substance abuse for each sport in the professional leagues. Whatever professional sport you decide to play, make sure that you are fully aware of their Substance abuse policy.

If you use any drugs or substances that are prohibited by the league, just remember that you will be tested for any and all substances banned by the NFL. The substance collector will show up. You know the person who collects the urine samples? Use good judgment; otherwise, you could very well put yourself and others in danger. Always follow your first GOOD mind. You are responsible for your own actions so MAKE WISE DECISIONS.

A FEW WORDS OF ENCOURAGEMENT

Some players choose to participate in professional sports for the wrong reasons. It might be for money or women. When you put those two together some men think they have the power to do whatever they want. This false sense of power can actually cause the desires for money and women to intensify. These athletes believe this false power will get them what they desire. Unfortunately, their desires and the material things they seek come to symbolize them. Don't fall into that trap. **If you are playing sports for the right reasons you will be a winner, even when the game is over.**

As a player you may not always get the stats or the media attention you want. But your teammates and coaches will see that you are blocking down the field to help your teammates, hustling down a tackle from the opposite side of the field, or making a touchdown. Whatever your sport, everything you do may not always show up on the stat sheets. Sometimes it's making the unselfish play that makes the biggest difference.

For whatever reason, not everyone will make it into the NFL, NBA, NHL, or MLB. Stay strong and remember that you do have a plan B. Stay ENCOURAGED not DISCOURAGED.

STAYING FOCUSED

Players who are focused will be confident. They will take good care of their bodies and will be careful about what they put into their bodies. They will be ready to play full speed and will give 110% at any given time. They will be able to go out, catch balls, block, tackle, make baskets, score goals, hit home runs or whatever is needed to help their team. A player who is not focused will not be ready. The plays might seem like a foreign language to them. They may be late for meetings and not concentrating in film study.

All players should try to help each other. Don't be afraid to give constructive criticism, and learn to accept constructive criticism. Pay attention to the best ways to communicate with your teammates. What will work with one teammate may not work with another.

Look out for your teammates. If you know a teammate has had too much to drink, there is a way to tell him without being too critical of them. DON"T LET THEM DRIVE! Stay aware of the people around your team, everybody is not a friend. Sometimes if a group of players goes out to dinner, the same person might always pick up the tab, even though other players make more money. If you are the person who continuously pays the bill, your teammates are taking advantage of you. Don't be taken advantage of and don't take advantage of your teammates. It's acceptable to pay occasionally, but not every time. You do not have to impress others by flashing your credit cards or your cash money.

PRAISE HIM

Celebrating is a time of rejoicing. Some people were taught to get on their knees to thank God for His goodness, His grace and His mercy. They THANK GOD for bringing them to where they are and for the victories they win. They have learned to glorify God so that He receives the credit.

Others celebrate by drinking alcohol, champagne or smoking cigars; to each his own. However, if you were taught to be thankful to God, DON'T EVER FORGET THAT. Always remember to BE YOURSELF. Don't think you have to drink and smoke to fit in. You can have fun, celebrate and enjoy yourself without smoking and drinking alcohol. There are non-alcoholic beverages available to you. If you don't drink, don't be afraid to say no.

If you are a member of a church, you should pay tithes, which is 10% of your income. If you are not, you can give offerings and donations if you would like. In tithing, you pay the tenth and keep 90% for yourself and pay your bills. The point is to pay God first. It's important that you give from the heart and not under compulsion. Make sure that before you give it has been placed on your heart to do so. You will know when to give, and to whom you are giving. Don't give because you want something in return.

Ever since my children started playing football and running track, whenever I see a player get injured, or see his or her face in the news or read something negative about them I automatically start praying for them. It doesn't matter who they are, because they are someone's child and someone's family member. I have done this for years and I still do. Seeing someone hurting doesn't give me any joy or satisfaction. My children have always been taught to pray for others, for their illnesses and for their successes. We pray for our finances, especially for those who handle them. There is so much to pray about, and it's a blessing to know someone is praying for you. We all need prayer.

Chapter 11

Lead Your Life

LEAD BY EXAMPLE

The most successful players lead by example. If you are able to work hard and achieve some of your dreams, make sure you pass on the best of what you have learned to our future generations. Young rookies watch everything veteran players do. If a veteran carries oneself as a professional, the rookies see and act accordingly.

No one is perfect. We all make mistakes, but when we do, we have to pick ourselves up, dust ourselves off, and get back in the race. Whether you are going through your daily activities or overcoming adversity, keep your head up and lead by example. You can make it to the top through hard work, discipline, positivity and good decisions – and what got you there, will keep you there. If you are a leader on your team, a veteran on a professional team, an older brother, sister or parent, start by respecting yourself and showing others the way to success through your actions.

REMEMBER...

THE "B" THEORY

- BE THE STRONGEST: You can be strong in certain areas, so work hard.

- BE THE FASTEST: You can be a fast learner, a fast runner

- BE THE SMARTEST: Use good judgment, and make wise decisions.

- BE THE BEST YOU CAN AT WHATEVER YOU DO.

HISTORY – HIS - STORY

Every step you take and everything you do in life is history. Everything you do is going to tell a story. What is your history? What will your actions say about you? Your story is being written and the true story will be told. Don't be afraid to make your dreams a reality and don't let anyone stop you. You can do it!

Part 2:

TO PRO PLAYBOOK/JOURNAL

PLAYBOOK/JOURNAL

_____

_____

_____

_____

_____

_____

_____

_____

_____

_____

_____

_____

_____

_____

PLAYBOOK/JOURNAL

_____

_____

_____

_____

_____

_____

_____

_____

_____

_____

_____

_____

_____

_____

PLAYBOOK/JOURNAL

_____

_____

_____

_____

_____

_____

_____

_____

_____

_____

_____

_____

_____

PLAYBOOK/JOURNAL

_____

_____

_____

_____

_____

_____

_____

_____

_____

_____

_____

_____

_____

_____

PLAYBOOK/JOURNAL

_____

_____

_____

_____

_____

_____

_____

_____

_____

_____

_____

_____

_____

_____

PLAYBOOK/JOURNAL

_____

_____

_____

_____

_____

_____

_____

_____

_____

_____

_____

_____

_____

_____

_____

PLAYBOOK/JOURNAL

_____

_____

_____

_____

_____

_____

_____

_____

_____

_____

_____

_____

_____

_____

PLAYBOOK/JOURNAL

_____

_____

_____

_____

_____

_____

_____

_____

_____

_____

_____

_____

_____

_____

PLAYBOOK/JOURNAL

_____

_____

_____

_____

_____

_____

_____

_____

_____

_____

_____

_____

_____

_____

PLAYBOOK/JOURNAL

PLAYBOOK/JOURNAL

_____

_____

_____

_____

_____

_____

_____

_____

_____

_____

_____

_____

_____

_____

PLAYBOOK/JOURNAL

_____

_____

_____

_____

_____

_____

_____

_____

_____

_____

_____

_____

_____

_____

PLAYBOOK/JOURNAL

_____

_____

_____

_____

_____

_____

_____

_____

_____

_____

_____

_____

_____

_____

PLAYBOOK/JOURNAL

_____

_____

_____

_____

_____

_____

_____

_____

_____

_____

_____

_____

_____

_____

PLAYBOOK/JOURNAL

_____

_____

_____

_____

_____

_____

_____

_____

_____

_____

_____

_____

_____

_____

PLAYBOOK/JOURNAL

_____

_____

_____

_____

_____

_____

_____

_____

_____

_____

_____

_____

_____

_____

PLAYBOOK/JOURNAL

PLAYBOOK/JOURNAL

PLAYBOOK/JOURNAL

_____

_____

_____

_____

_____

_____

_____

_____

_____

_____

_____

_____

_____

PLAYBOOK/JOURNAL

_____

_____

_____

_____

_____

_____

_____

_____

_____

_____

_____

_____

_____

_____

_____